Acknowledgment

Is It Fair? - Learning About Equal Oppurtunities was originally commissioned by Martin Patrick of the Humberside Partnership. The idea was to produce an activity pack for children of primary school age addressing the subject of equal opportunities. The project was initially intended to be on a smaller scale, but soon grew as I realised just how integral the idea of equal opportunities is in so many areas of life. I would like to thank Martin for his support and encouragement throughout the devising and writing of the pack, as well as Richard Jessop of the Humberside Partnership for his help with the initial design and format of the pack.

Sarah Johnston

4

LIVEWIRE GRAPHICS

Charles Dickens's

Great Expectations

TEACHER'S RESOURCE BOOK

EDITED BY
Philip Page and Marilyn Pettit

ILLUSTRATED BY
Philip Page

Published in association with

The Basic Skills Agency

Hodder & Stoughton

A MEMBER OF THE HODDER HEADLINE GROUP

Acknowledgements
The publisher would like to thank the following copyright holders for permission to reproduce their photographs:
p.1 Head and shoulders engraving of Charles Dickens (1812–70) by W.G. Jackman © Bettman/CORBIS;
pp.9, 20, 39, 50, 57, 58 © bfi Collections; p.36 © Topham Picturepoint.

Orders: please contact Bookpoint Ltd, 130 Milton Park, Abingdon, Oxon OX14 4SB. Telephone: (44) 01235 827720
Fax: (44) 01235 400454. Lines are open from 9.00–6.00, Monday to Saturday, with a 24 hour message answering service.
You can also order through our website: *www.hodderheadline.co.uk*

British Library Cataloguing in Publication Date
A catalogue record for this title is available from the British Library

ISBN 0 340 87165 2

First Published   2003
Impression number   10 9 8 7 6 5 4 3 2 1
Year   2007 2006 2005 2004 2003

Text Copyright © 2003 Philip Page and Marilyn Pettit

Cover illustration by Dave Smith.
Typeset by Fakenham Photosetting Limited, Fakenham, Norfolk.
Printed in Great Britain for Hodder & Stoughton Educational, a division of Hodder Headline, 338 Euston Road, London
NW1 3BH by Hobbs the Printers, Totton, Hants.

Contents

Introduction

The activities in this Teacher's Resource Book are intended to be used with *Livewire Graphics: Great Expectations*. All references, such as page numbers, relate to that book.

The tasks directly address the pupils, so that, where appropriate, there is opportunity for pupil autonomy. However, the majority of the tasks lend themselves to teacher/pupil/class interaction and it is important that the activities are seen as opportunities for such interaction. The tasks differ, in that some might be completed in one lesson, whereas others might last over a number of lessons.

It must be stressed that the activities are not intended to be used as worksheets.

There are a variety of activities, so that pupils experience:

- collaborative and individual work
- drama – both rehearsed and improvised
- a wide range of written responses in different genres
- debate and discussion, encompassing a range of issues
- exploration of language, with reference to both Dickens's use of language and today's English.

The tasks have been devised with the National Curriculum requirements in mind. The English Framework, with its clear emphasis on learning objectives and the four language modes is firmly embedded in the activities.

Pupils are encouraged to consider the social and historical issues surrounding the text, as well as considering Charles Dickens and his time. The emphasis is on fun, challenge and engagement, where pupils learn to support others and evaluate their work, so that they have clear targets for improvement.

Charles Dickens – not just an author

Read the facts in note form below. Your task is to use these facts and any others you find from your research to write Dickens's obituary. An obituary appears in a newspaper following a person's death. It gives information about the person and 'celebrates' the person's achievements. Before writing, read some in class, highlighting the characteristic features.

- Born: 7 February 1812, Portsmouth
- Author of numerous books inc. *Great Expectations*, *Oliver Twist*, *A Christmas Carol*
- Also worked as journalist and Editor of *Daily News*
- Ambition to be an actor. Failed to attend audition in Covent Garden – had cold!
- Performed in amateur groups. Gave public readings
- Walked long distances alone or with friends, also traveller – America and Europe
- Married Catherine Hogarth 1836, separated 1858. May have had a mistress: Ellen Ternan
- Fathered ten children
- Died 9 June 1870, Kent

Think about your lead line. It needs to reflect the importance of Dickens and the loss to the world of writing.

1

Setting the atmosphere

Read the first two pages of the pupil's book.

1 To form an impression of the tone and atmosphere that Dickens is trying to set, answer the following questions:

Which is the first sentence that makes you think the novel might not be a completely happy one?

What is it about the phrase 'the marsh country' that makes the setting seem eerie?

How does the location of this scene make the reader feel uneasy?

What shocks the reader when Pip answers the question, 'Where's your mother?'

How do the convict's threats make you feel? How did they affect Pip?

2 Imagine that you are the director or producer of the film *Great Expectations*. You want a frightening opening, one that is going to make the viewer sit on the edge of his seat!

Discuss, in pairs, what your first 2 minutes of film will contain.

Think about: the location, the geographical area, the appearance of the convict.

Think about: camera angles, close-ups, the lighting.

Draw a storyboard that will explain your opening scene.

Be prepared to explain your choices to other pairs in your class.

3 What conclusions have you reached about this opening scene and the way in which the opening shots can set the atmosphere?

Violence and threats

Dialogue is an important device for setting scenes and giving readers information about characters.

1 In pairs, make up a two-minute script that sets the scene for your audience, for example, read the few lines below and decide where the two characters are, how you know and what you learn about them:

> A: I hate this place. What are you here for?
>
> B: I've had this awful cough. I thought I'd better get it checked out. What about you?
>
> A: Me? Oh I've come for a blood test! I'm a bit scared!

What about this one:

> A: Have you got any in a size 4? I'm fed up of walking round now.
>
> B: I'll just go and look. If we haven't got any in that colour, do you want the white pair?

Perform your own for another pair and see how long it takes them to guess the setting and give some information about your characters.

2 In pairs, read page 2 again – one being the convict, the other Pip. What do you notice about the pace of the dialogue? What does that add to the scene?
Think about the words: *interrogatives* and *commands*. How do these types of sentences make Pip and the reader feel?
How does the convict deliver his most fierce threats – whispering or shouting at Pip? Which is the more effective tone of voice?

3 If someone were to ask you this – 'I'm thinking of reading *Great Expectations* – what's the beginning like?' – rehearse the answer you would give and be ready to say it out loud to your group. Do you all have the same impressions of the beginning?

Table manners

1 Read page 3. Pip is trying to sneak food out for the *'dreadful acquaintance and the still more dreadful young man'*.
At last, he decides to put his bread and butter down the leg of his trousers.
Even though Pip isn't feeling happy and even though the readers might share his fear, we still see the funny side of this scene.
This type of humour is *slapstick,* because it involves mess!
What about other forms of slapstick: clowns with water, slipping on bananas – what others can you think of?

2 Have you ever been in a situation where you really haven't liked the food that you've been given, but you know it would be rude to leave it on your plate? Perhaps at a friend's house or at a relative's, or some special friends' of your parents? Tell your partner what happened, then share these experiences with the class.

3 Imagine you have been invited to your Auntie's house. Your parents have told you to be polite. You sit at the table and you are faced with food that makes you feel ill just looking at it. What are you going to do? You can't push your plate away and say, 'Yuck! That looks disgusting! I'm not eating THAT!'
Write a short amusing account of the episode, using slapstick and exaggeration!

4 Read it aloud to a partner to evaluate the effectiveness of your comical piece.

Tickler!

1 Tickler first shows up on page 3.
In the original, Pip's sister has been out 13 times looking for Pip and Joe says:
'What's worse, she's got Tickler with her.'
Pip goes on to add: *Tickler was a wax-ended piece of cane, worn smooth by collision with my tickled frame.*
When his sister returns, she catches Pip, and we are told that she *'applied Tickler'* and, *'concluded by throwing me at Joe'*.
What do you think of this violent treatment?

2 Using your library, find further details on the treatment of children during the time Dickens wrote. Your teacher will help you locate information.

3 Using your notes, prepare a short presentation on this subject. You might want to use PowerPoint to illustrate your points.

4 Once you have presented your piece, be prepared to contribute to a whole class discussion. This discussion will debate the saying:
Spare the rod, and spoil the child.
Before contributing, talk in small groups about the types of punishment that children have had to endure and perhaps some of them still have to put up with. This will help you gather other opinions.

5 Following your discussion, can you finish the saying: **Spare the rod, and** ... so that it has a less violent message?

If you had the choice . . .

1 When have you said: There's nothing to eat in this house! There's never anything nice to eat! I just fancy some___, but we haven't got any! I'm hungry but I don't know what to have.
Some of those lines might make your parents cross. Why? What might they answer?

2 The convict has no choice when it comes to food. He has to eat what Pip brings him.
Read page 4 to find out what food Pip stole for the convict.

3 If you had the choice of eating whatever you wanted, what would you choose?
Write your choice down in the form of a menu. Remember to add adjectives and adjectival phrases that will make the reader's mouth water!
To help you, read the menu below, highlighting the words and phrases that describe the food:

> A creamy, piping hot bowl of genuine home-made mushroom soup

> A deliciously crispy fresh bowl of salad, with a tasty vegetable pie, topped with featherweight pastry

> A tangy, light, heavenly ice-cream, delicately topping a dish of newly-picked succulent strawberries

4 Why does that sound better than: tinned soup, heated in a microwave, followed by a pie with salad, and to finish – ice-cream and strawberries?

5 Swap work and discuss what features make your piece effective.

Escaped and recaptured

1 Where might you hear the following and who might be speaking?

- Today at approximately 6 a.m. a prisoner was reported missing from one of the Hulks. Soldiers have warned people to lock their doors and on no account approach this dangerous man.
- I didn't exactly see him. I mean it was misty, but I know I heard something out in the yard and when I peered into the mist I could make out an evil shape.
- All our men, those who serve the King, are ready to begin the search. Trust me, the prisoners won't last long on those marshes. We'll have them back in chains this very night.
- Our prison ships have an excellent safety record. We have never lost a prisoner! This has been an unfortunate incident, but there will be a full investigation of our security systems. We put public safety above all else.

> an eyewitness   a soldier
> a spokesperson for the prisons   a reporter

2 What features of each text helped you to decide who spoke the words?

3 Now read pages 7 and 8. The convicts are recaptured by the soldiers.

What devices are used in these headlines that might appear in a newspaper reporting this story?

Courageous soldiers capture convicts!

Quick marsh – convicts get their comeuppance

Safe and sound behind bars

Hide and Seek! Capturing convicts child's play for our soldier lads

Escaped and recaptured continued

1 Imagine that you are a television reporter who is on the scene when the convicts are recaptured. Write down your words for the viewers. Rehearse them before you deliver them to your class. You might begin:

> Behind me, you can see the soldiers dragging out from what looks to be a ditch, the two escaped convicts ...

2 Write the front page sensational story of the recapture of the convicts! Your newspaper is a tabloid, keen to praise the soldiers and remind its readers of the evils the convicts are guilty of.

Before writing, remind yourself of the language and format used in front page stories. Remind yourself of the details by reading pages 7 and 8. Don't forget: the marshes, the weather, what drew the soldiers to the convicts, the possible eye-witnesses, the final destination for the convicts.

Remember to include information that answers: When? Where? Who? What? Why?

3 Make up your own headline using a technique that will draw your readers in.

4 When finished, print out your 'story'. Make a display of front-page reports and decide which ones catch the readers' eyes. Make sure you have your reasons before reporting to the class on your choice.

The marshes – descriptive writing

1 At the beginning of *Great Expectations* there are a number of descriptions of the marshes. Read the lines below and answer the questions that follow. This will help you to study the writer's craft – that is the way in which he sets the scene – by using descriptive techniques. You might want to work with a partner.

I found out that ... the dark flat wilderness beyond the churchyard, intersected with dykes and mounds and gates, with scattered cattle feeding on it, was the marshes; and that the low leaden line beyond, was the river; and that the distant savage lair from which the wind was rushing, was the sea; and that the small bundle of shivers growing afraid of it all and beginning to cry, was Pip.

2 What effect does the adjective *'dark'* and the noun *'wilderness'* have on the reader? The *'wilderness'* combined with the *'churchyard'* makes another impression on the reader – what is it?

3 The enumeration of *'dykes and mounds and gates'* might suggest a never-ending landscape. How might this create an uneasy feeling in the reader?

4 What do you make of the adjective *'scattered'* when it describes the cattle?

5 The alliteration in *'low leaden line'* slows the pace of the phrase. Why is this effective?

6 What lives in a *'lair'* and why is it appropriate to use the adjective *'savage'* here? Is it also appropriate to describe the sea using this metaphor? What does it tell you about the sea?

7 Pip is writing his story in the first person singular, and yet he distances himself at one point, using the third person, saying he is a *'small bundle of shivers'* and he refers to himself as Pip. What effect does this have?

The marshes – descriptive writing continued

8 The writer uses the words 'and' / 'and that' a number of times. How does this help us to sympathise with Pip?

9 What visual images strike you as being the most frightening and why?

10 Now read another description of the marshes and answer the questions, by discussing with a partner:

> The marshes were just a long black horizontal line ... and the river was just another horizontal line ... the sky was just a row of long angry red lines and dense black lines intermixed. On the edge of the river I could faintly make out the only two black things in all the prospect ... the beacon by which the sailors steered – like an unhooped cask upon a pole – the other, a gibbet with some chains hanging to it which had once held a pirate.

What do the colours *'black'* and *'red'* suggest to you? They symbolise certain ideas/concepts. Are the colours suitable for the scene? Why?

What effect do the adjectives *'angry'* and *'dense'* have, when used to describe colours?

Find the simile and explain why it is an effective one.

What is a *'gibbet'*? What does its presence add to the atmosphere?

What do you think happened to the *'pirate'*, considering that the *'chains'* now hang there, empty?

11 Write a description of a hostile landscape of your own using some of these techniques.

Miss Havisham – the recluse

1 Look up the word 'recluse' in the dictionary. In what way is Miss Havisham a recluse?

2 There have been many people in the past and some in the present too who have lived and still live a reclusive lifestyle.
As a class, with the teacher, come up with the names of some of those people. To help you, think about: a famous pop star of today; a famous pop singer from Sweden; a millionaire who lived in America.

3 Why do some people prefer to live life almost alone? Would you like to live like that? Share with a partner times when you have wanted to be alone. How long did that feeling last and what made you decide to rejoin your family/friends?

4 What has made Miss Havisham refuse to mix with others?
Read page 10. Pip sees her for the first time. Now read the original text below:

> She was dressed in satins, and lace, and silks – all of white. Her shoes were white. And she had a long white veil from her hair, and she had bridal flowers in her hair, but her hair was white. Some bright jewels sparkled on her neck and on her hands, and some other jewels lay sparkling on the table. Dresses and half-packed trunks were scattered about. She had but one shoe on – her veil was but half arranged, her watch and chain were not put on ... her handkerchief, and gloves, and some flowers, and a prayer-book, all confusedly heaped about the looking-glass. Everything was faded and yellow ... the figure was skin and bone. Once I had been taken to see some ghastly wax-work at the Fair, once I had been taken to one of our old marsh churches to see a skeleton that had been dug out of a vault. Now, wax-work and skeleton seemed to have dark eyes that moved and looked at me.

Miss Havisham – the recluse
continued

5 This description would not be out of place in a horror story. What features of horror does this piece of text have?

In the opening three lines on the previous page, bridal items and her white hair are placed alongside each other. Juxtaposing these suggests that things aren't right. Why?

Why do the *'half-packed trunks'* make Pip and the reader feel slightly nervous?

In what way does the word *'scattered'* make the reader think that things aren't 'normal' in this room?

She has one shoe on! Can you explain why that appears creepy?

How does the writer convey decay?

If Dickens had written the last line without mentioning the fair and the vault, the description wouldn't have been as frightening. Can you explain why this is so?

6 Read page 10 again. The pose that Miss Havisham has – sitting in *'an armchair, with an elbow resting on the table and her head leaning on that hand'* – is a position we have all sat in. Usually we are relaxing when we do this. We know now that she wasn't relaxing – why did Dickens throw us off our guard?

7 Write your description of a 'strange person' from the viewpoint of one who is meeting him/her for the first time. Try to make it scary and unnerving for the reader. You can use some of the techniques Dickens used, but your words must be your own.

Plan your piece carefully, before you begin. Once you have finished, let your partner read your text. Offering positive criticism helps writers improve their style.

Your first impressions of Estella

1 Read pages 10, 11 and 12. In pairs, jot down your first impressions of this young girl.

2 Go over the text once more. Think about the following:
Pip is being polite when he says *'After you miss'*, but she makes fun of him and refers to Pip as *'boy'*. What does that tell us about her attitude to him? Later on, she is amazed that Miss Havisham should ask her to play cards with *'This boy!'* Why is she so shocked?
How do her words: *'He is a common labouring-boy'* add to your answer?
She insults his use of language – how? What doesn't she like about him that tells her he works hard for a living?
Pip thinks she is *'very proud, very pretty, very insulting'* – what would you have said if you were Pip?
She treats him as if he is an animal. Find the evidence of this.
Find evidence of the fact that Estella takes pleasure from his pain.

3 Turn to page 11. How do you think Miss Havisham is going to 'use' Estella ? What might have happened to Miss Havisham to make her want Estella to do this to Pip? Remember she is dressed in white, has bridal flowers in her hair and admits she has a broken heart.

4 Does Estella seem happy to be manipulated in this way?

Satis House

1 What word do you know beginning with 'satis' and what does it mean?

2 Estella tells Pip, *'it meant when it was given, that whoever had this house, could want for nothing else.'*
The description of the house suggests there has been a change from the time it was given.
The house helps us to understand the occupiers. Read the extracts from the original text.

> The great front entrance had two chains across it … Miss Havisham's house had a great many iron bars. Some of the windows had been walled up; of those that remained, all the lower were rustily barred.

What other building has so many bars and chains?

> All was empty and disused. The cold wind seemed to blow colder there, than outside the gate; and it made a shrill noise in howling in and out at the open sides of the brewery, like the noise of wind in the rigging of a ship at sea.

'Shrill' is not a pleasant adjective, but coupled with howling, it appears worse – why? What animal does 'howling' bring to mind? In what way might a ship at sea suggest loneliness and isolation? Is this appropriate?

> No pigeons in the dove-cot, no horses in the stable, no pigs in the sty, no malt in the storehouse, no smells of grains and beer in the copper or the vat.

What does the repetition of the word 'no' suggest to you?
The overall impression of Satis House is not one of satisfaction, but just the opposite: dissatisfaction.

3 Using the above examples and details on pages 10 and 12, explain in writing why it seems from the description of the house that the occupants are dissatisfied.

Playing games

1 What games did you used to play when you were younger? Which of these involved running, chasing, hiding, or perhaps just sitting down?

Make a list with your partner. Choose one of the games and write a set of instructions that explain how to play the game of your choice. Give it to another pair so that they can check how easy the instructions are to follow.

Ask older people – relatives/friends – what games they used to play. Compare with the class and make a Top Ten list of games.

2 In Victorian times, many poor children played in the streets. Games that we have today were popular then: dominoes, marbles, skipping.

Do you know any or can you find some skipping songs? They often sound like rhymes.

Victorian children had entertainment: Punch and Judy shows, street magicians and clowns.

They also went to the Penny Gaff – this was a type of theatre, costing a penny to go in. There would be singing and dancing here.

3 Estella and Pip play cards. Using your library and the Internet, research into Victorian games, including card games. Choose one and present it to the class in the form of a spoken piece, explaining how it is played.

4 Miss Havisham and Estella also play another 'game' – what is it? Do you think there will be a winner?

That's a bit over the top!

1 What do people mean when they say this? Take for example:

> You're dressed a bit over the top. We're only going to the local pub.

> You didn't need to go over the top and shout at him. He was only trying his best.

> Don't go over the top with the details. We know you're making it up!

2 Remind yourself of what happened at Satis House by reading pages 10, 11 and 12.

Now read page 13 – Pip's exaggerated account of what happened. In this he goes 'over the top'!

How does he describe Miss Havisham?

What details does Pip choose to show that Miss Havisham is rich?

Why does he bother to tell these lies?

3 What does the piece below exaggerate?

> Well ... I was walking in the park, when I heard this terrible screech. I looked up and saw a huge dragon, with burning eyes and flaming nostrils swoop down from the sky. It opened its fiery mouth and was just about to shoot flames at two little girls. I raced towards them, jumped on top of them, protecting them from the dragon, who was so angry that he turned away and flew off into the clouds. That's how I cut my hands and knees and ripped my trousers Mum.

4 Think of an ordinary event – perhaps going on holiday, going shopping, a visitor calling at your house. Write a piece that will exaggerate the event and impress your friends.

An apprentice

1 What do you understand by this word? Read pages 19 and 20. Find out what the word 'indentures' means and how it applies to Joe and Pip. What might Miss Havisham mean by 'a premium'? Pip didn't want to continue with this trade – he wanted to become a gentleman!

2 There were many unpleasant jobs that children did. Read the list below and find out what the jobs entailed: streetsellers, chimney sweeps/climbing boys, mudlarks, working in the coal mines or the factories, going into service.

- 1833 Factory Act banned children under 9 from working in factories and mills
- 1842 children under 10 banned from working in mines
- 1844 Factory Act limited the working day for 9–13 year olds to six and a half hours
- 1875 using climbing boys was banned.

We also learn of other jobs in *Great Expectations*: Joe is a blacksmith, Pip visits the tailor, the hatter, the bootmaker and the hosier.
Find out what these trades involved. Do we have anything similar today?

3 If you could go back in time, say to 1832, and have an appointment with the Prime Minister, what would you say to him to make him do something about the conditions in which children worked?
Prepare your speech so that you convince him to act! Remember to discuss as a class the features of an effective persuasive speech!

Collecting the facts and giving evidence

1 Page 22 and 23 give an account of what happened to Mrs Joe Gargery. Read these again.

Collect the evidence and put it down in note form, for example:

> Victim on kitchen floor. Hit on back of head by heavy object.

2 Read this extract from the original text. It adds more detail. Make more notes on the attack.

> Joe had been at the Three Jolly Bargemen from a quarter after eight o'clock to a quarter before ten. While he was there, my sister had been seen standing at the kitchen door, and had exchanged Good Night with a farm-labourer going home. The man could not be more particular as to the time at which he saw her, than it must have been before nine. When Joe went home at five minutes before ten, he found her struck down on the floor, and promptly called in assistance. The fire had not then burnt unusually low, nor was the snuff of the candle very long; the candle, however, had been blown out.
>
> Nothing had been taken away from any part of the house. Neither was there any disarrangement of the kitchen. She had been struck with something blunt and heavy, on the head and spine; after the blows were dealt, something heavy had been thrown down at her with considerable violence, as she lay on her face.

3 Imagine you are a member of the police force. You have to present this evidence to a Court of Law. You will do this by presenting to the class. Rehearse your evidence to make sure you can use your notes as prompts when you are speaking.

Listen to the comments. These will help you improve your work.

It's all off!

1 Read page 30. The line: *'The day came but not the bridegroom'* tells us that Miss Havisham was let down by her fiancé at the last minute.

The phrases: 'let down' and 'all off' both tell us that a relationship is over.

Can you think of other words that convey this meaning? To start you off – dumped, ditched …

2 Research into the ways in which people use mobile phones tells us that many people are 'dumped' by text. Write the text message that the bridegroom might have sent Miss Havisham on their wedding day. Remember to use text language / abbreviations.

To help you, read the one below that is from one friend to another, postponing a meeting.

> Soz. Can't make mtg. Thort cud but imposs. Mite b abl to make 2mro. Ring 2 tel me wat goin on.

3 Now write two short letters – one that Miss Havisham receives from her fiancé, in which he tries not to hurt her; the other sparing no thoughts for her feelings whatsoever.

Remember the layout of a letter. The style would be formal, because he is distancing himself from her.

4 Compare your letters with your partner's. Join up with another pair, and explain what you liked about the letters and what could have been improved. By nominating a spokesperson, report your ideas to the whole class.

Watch out – she'll get you!

Parents often warn their children about places by telling them stories, for example, some people say that *Little Red Riding Hood* and *Goldilocks* were stories told to frighten children so that they wouldn't wander off.

Some parents pretend to ring up Father Christmas or the Naughty Police when children behave badly, so that they quickly change their behaviour, because they are worried they won't get presents!

1 With a partner, share any experiences you might have had or heard of.

2 Imagine you are a parent who is worried about your child playing near Satis House. It looks a dangerous place and you know that a strange woman and child live there! Using page 30, retell Miss Havisham's story as if you are telling it to a child as a warning that s/he must not play there.

You can then perform your story as a reading for your class.

3 Now retell it as if you are a child explaining to another child. You will need to think about your vocabulary choices.

You might begin: 'We can't go up there to play, because my mum told me …'

4 With a partner, compare your use of language in both retellings.

The Pocket Family

Pip meets his tutor on page 31. In the original text, the family is described in detail. It is a caring family, who provide a contrast to the other 'families' in the novel. Before reading the extract, discuss two 'families' in the novel: Pip, Joe and Mrs Joe/Miss Havisham and Estella.

1 Now read the extract from the original. Highlight the positive features that Dickens writes about. Discuss the contrast Dickens wanted to bring out by using this ideal scene.

> Mrs Pocket was sitting on a garden chair, reading, with her legs upon another garden chair; and two nursemaids were looking about them while the children played. 'Master Alick and Miss Jane,' cried one of the nurses to two of the children, 'if you go a bouncing up against the bushes, you'll fall over into the river and be drownded, and what'll your pa say then!' ... there were no fewer than six little Pockets ... I had scarcely arrived when a seventh could be heard. 'If there ain't Baby!' Mrs Pocket danced the infant a little in her lap, while the other children played about it.

What supports the fact that the family are: relaxed, easy-going, playful, caring, interested in each other?

2 Write down at least 5 adjectives and adjectival phrases to describe a happy family grouping. Give them to your partner, who has 3 minutes to rehearse a spoken description of a happy family scene, using these phrases or using scenes that illustrate these qualities in a family. He can use quick notes to prompt him, but no more. After 3 minutes he has to present this snapshot scene of a happy family.

Invitations

There are many types of invitations – to a wedding, a funeral, a party, etc.

1 Read the texts below and decide whether these are formal or informal and what relationship the speaker and the person/s addressed might have.

- Oi, d'you wanna come round to my house tonight? The house'll be empty and we can have a laugh.
- You are cordially invited to attend the Achievements Ceremony at High Top School, where your daughter will be receiving a special award.
- Mr and Mrs Barnfield request the pleasure of Mr and Mrs Morris at the wedding of their daughter Ruth to . . .
- Hi gang! You're all invited to have a drink at my place to celebrate. My final exams are over!

2 On page 32, Pip receives an invitation to dine with Mr Jaggers. This might have been written on a card – probably an expensive card. Design the invitation, keeping the language formal. In the original text, Jaggers says: 'No ceremony and no dinner dress'. Guests were to arrive at Gerrard-street, Soho at 6 p.m.

Making excuses and letting down friends

1 As he matures, Pip behaves badly on a number of occasions. Read pages 33 and 34.

Biddy writes a letter to Pip, informing him that Joe is coming to London and will meet him. What is Pip's reaction to this and why? It turns out that Joe has come to deliver a message to Pip from Miss Havisham. He has put himself out for Pip and Pip isn't grateful! What textual evidence is there that tells the readers Joe is not comfortable in London with Pip? How do we know that Joe realizes Pip doesn't want to be seen with him.

2 On page 33 Pip says, *'If I could have kept him away by paying money, I certainly would have paid money.'*

If Pip had had a telephone, he might have called Biddy or Joe and made some excuse. Perhaps he would have claimed he was going away, or that he was ill.

In pairs, script the telephone conversation that Pip has with Biddy first. Imagine that Biddy suspects Pip is telling lies. Continue the script from the point where Biddy might say, 'I think you'd better tell Joe yourself. He's here now. I'm handing the phone to him.'

3 Act out your script for the class. Remember not to look at each other and to use your tone of voice, pauses and silence to make your meaning clear.

Deepest sympathy

1 One of the most difficult letters to write must be one that informs a person of a death.

Read page 36 where Pip receives a letter, informing him of his sister's death.

This might have been the letter:

> Honoured Sir,
>
> We beg to inform you that your dearly beloved sister, Mrs Joe Gargery, has sadly departed this world. It is with deep regret that we have to inform you that Mrs Joe Gargery passed over on Monday last at twenty minutes past six in the evening.
>
> Your attendance is requested at the internment, which will take place on Monday next at three o'clock in the afternoon.
>
> TRABB & CO.

2 We learn on page 36 that Pip sends a letter to Joe. Write this letter, expressing your sadness at the loss. Let him know that you will be attending the funeral. Perhaps you might want to give him some words of encouragement.

3 On the same page we read that, 'my sister was laid quietly in the earth.' – in other words buried. When writing to soften the event and to make hard things easier to bear people often use *euphemisms*. Read these euphemisms often used when someone has died: 'passed to the other side', 'gone to a better place', 'gone to meet her Maker', 'sitting by God's throne'.

What might these euphemisms refer to: 'ethnic cleansing', 'late night disturbances', 'freedom fighters', 'fallen off the back of a lorry', 'in the clink', 'eating for two'. Find two more of your own. Make a class display that shows how rich our language is.

These are my instructions

1 Read page 14. Pip calls at the Three Jolly Bargemen on his way from school to fetch Joe Gargery. A stranger gives him what Pip thinks is a shilling, but it turns out to be two one-pound notes. In order to deliver the money, Magwitch must have given the stranger precise instructions on what to do.

Write out the instructions and remember Magwitch would have wanted it done right!

To help you, think about the following: the stranger needs to know the name of the pub; he'll need to be able to spot Joe (how would you describe Joe – strong? He should be because he's a blacksmith! He smokes a pipe!); he'll have to make sure he gets the right boy; he will also need to show Pip something that reminds him of the convict and he'll need to do this so that no one else sees.

2 Magwitch also gives Jaggers, the lawyer, instructions. Use pages 26, 27 and 38 to write the list of instructions the convict would have written for Jaggers. In writing these instructions, try to use today's English rather than the language Jaggers used in the nineteenth century.

And you thought Magwitch a villain!

1 What crimes was Magwitch guilty of? Read page 43 to help you. Remind yourself of the link with Miss Havisham by reading page 30.

2 In the original text, Magwitch adds this:

> Compeyson's business was swindling, handwriting forging, stolen bank-note passing and such-like ... me and Compeyson was committed on a charge of putting stolen notes in circulation ... when the evidence was giv, I noticed how it was always me that the money had been paid to, how it was always me that had seemed to work the thing and get the profit ... and when it come to character, warn't it Compeyson as had been to school and warn't it him as had been know'd by witnesses in such clubs and societies ... and when we're sentenced ain't it him as gets seven year and me fourteen ...

What does this suggest happened to Magwitch? What does this tell you about status, connections and the class system?

3 There have been other fictional Victorian villains. Find out about Sweeney Todd – the barber! What about Mr Hyde (Dr Jekyll), Frankenstein's monster, Dracula?
Then there were real-life villains. Find out about Jack the Ripper and Mary Ann Cotton.
Films have been made based on the crimes of such villains!

4 Why do you think audiences enjoy being horrified by these criminals who commit vile crimes? Why are we so eager to be frightened by these people and events? Think about good / evil; fact/fiction.
Talk with a partner and share your ideas with the class.

Scripting a conversation

Read page 46. It is here that we learn of the danger to Magwitch and Wemmick's plan.

Pip has returned to London and has been given a note from Wemmick. What does it say and why has Wemmick warned Pip?

When Pip goes to see Wemmick, he explains what he has planned with Mr Herbert.

Working with a partner, script the conversation that must have taken place between Wemmick and Mr Herbert. In order to help you perform it, remember to use conventions, like stage directions that indicate how to deliver lines and how to use body language. Remember Wemmick never lets on that he definitely knows about Magwitch.

You might begin:

> **Wemmick**: (*looking over his shoulder*) Mr Herbert Sir, I have reason to believe that you have a certain man – we will mention no names – who might be a visitor of some sort, staying perhaps with Mr Pip.

> **Mr Herbert**: (*hesitating*) That might be the case! But I am not sure what this might have to do with you, even if it were true.

> **Wemmick**: If there were such a man, and if he were being watched by another, then it would be better if this man were to be moved wouldn't you say Sir?

He's behind you!

1 We learn on page 48 that Mr Wopsle is performing in a 'comic Christmas panto'.
What pantomimes have you seen and at what time of the year have you been to watch them?

2 In groups, list the typical ingredients of a pantomime. Report back to the class.

3 Read the facts below and answer the questions.

- Most pantomimes are based on traditional stories. Name at least three.
- They are divided into Acts and Scenes. What might the opening scene from *Cinderella* contain?
- Pantomimes have stock characters, for example: dames, principal boys/heroes, principal girls/beautiful heroines, a fairy godmother, a villain. Can you name any of these in the pantos you have seen? What have you noticed about the dame and the principal boy?
- Pantos have conventions (regular features). When might you shout, 'He's behind you!'
- When would you expect a character to answer, 'Oh no he isn't!' and what would the audience shout in return? What does an audience do when the villain appears on stage?
- A panto always has a happy ending – problems and complications are resolved. Give an example of a happy ending.
- Who said the following and in what pantomime:
  You SHALL go to the Ball!
  Fee Fie Fo Fum, I smell the blood of an Englishman.
  I am the Genie of the Lamp!
  To London to make my fortune!

  What other sayings can you challenge your partner with?

He's behind you! continued

4 In groups, choose a traditional story e.g. *Cinderella*, *Jack and the Beanstalk*, *Puss in Boots*, *Aladdin*. You are going to work together to write the first two scenes, so you need to know the story well.
Plan the outline of your two scenes – the characters, the action and where it takes place.

Note the way in which scripts are written to show characters how the lines should be spoken. Stage directions are given in brackets. Adverbs are used to indicate tone or pace. Phrases can show body language and facial movements.

Take for example *Cinderella*:

> **Cinders**: (*on knees scrubbing the hard stone floor*) I'm so tired ... I just want to stop and rest.
>
> **Buttons**: Hey Cinderella (*cheerfully bouncing onto stage*) the Prince is having a Ball to find a wife!

What do you notice about the stage directions and the punctuation cues?

When you have your outline, write your script as a group – all contributing to the piece.
Take turns to act as scribe.
Once finished, rehearse your scenes, ready to perform for your class.
If you are really successful, perhaps you could finish your pantomime and perform it for your Primary School.

Writing a telegram

Read page 51. We are told that the surgeon will write to Estella, who is in Paris, to let her know of Miss Havisham's injuries.

Rather than write a letter, it would have been quicker to send a telegram.

Read what might have been the surgeon's letter and using the information, write the telegram. Remember that telegrams give only the necessary information. They do not have to read in full sentences, as long as the sense is clear.

My dear lady,

It is my sad duty to have to inform you of an accident that has occurred at Satis House. Miss Havisham has sustained serious injuries, resulting in burns to the greater part of her body. It was extremely lucky that the young Mr Pip was able to douse the flames with his coats, otherwise the injuries would have been much worse. He also sustained burns to both his hands. No doubt you will want to return to Satis House to be with Miss Havisham. I will keep you informed,

Yours,

Performing a monologue

What does the prefix *mono* signify? You will know that the word monologue refers to a dramatic piece that is performed by one person.

1 Miss Havisham spends long periods of time on her own. She rejects society and as the story goes on, she begins to have regrets. Imagine that you are Miss Havisham. You will need to try and 'get in role' – that is understand her character and her motivation. Remember: body language, tone and pace.

Just before the fire, on page 51, imagine she has the chance to talk things through while she is alone. What she says will be delivered as a monologue.

In order to help you, the page numbers are included.

You may use the frame below to help you formulate your thoughts.

Supporting Frame
I had a reason for sending for Pip and introducing him to Estella. The first time ... (pages 10, 11, 12)
The second time I spoke to Pip of ... (pages 15, 16, 17)
Perhaps I did some good when I sent for Gargery to ... (pages 19, 20)
And later on, I learnt from him that he was to go ... (page 27)
And now, finally, I realize what I have done ... (page 50)

2 When you have finished, rehearse your piece, ready to perform in front of your class.

Formalities

Miss Havisham explains who brought Estella to her and why she wanted her. Remind yourself of this on page 50. On page 52, Jaggers carefully tells Pip something of what might have taken place.

1 Before Miss Havisham could have adopted Estella, certain formalities would have had to be undertaken.

- Instructions from Miss Havisham to Jaggers
- A letter from Jaggers to Miss Havisham
- An adoption certificate
- A signed statement by Estella's mother agreeing never to contact her daughter

2 Read the lines below and decide from which document they come:

I solemnly swear on this day and month never to …

Legal Guardian:

I charge you with the task of finding me a …

I am pleased to be able to inform you that I have …

Your teacher will be able to model more of the appropriate language used in these documents.

3 Choose one of the above and write it in a suitable style and format. Make a class display of these, so that the different forms are clear.

A miserable childhood

Pip was lucky. He survived childhood and grew up into a gentleman. Not all Victorian children were so lucky.

1 Read the facts below and add to them by researching in your library. Prepare to present your findings in the form of a talk to another class who might be about to study this novel or perhaps to your history teacher, who might be able to give you even more detail.

- Many babies were murdered (they were expensive to keep). Police found bodies in the Thames, in ponds, under railway bridges, on doorsteps.
- Often parents couldn't afford to keep their children so they sold them! Very often these children were neglected and died of starvation.
- The houses of the poorest people (slums) had no running water so many children died because water from a well or the river was contaminated.
- Many children were made to work almost as soon as they could walk. They made match-boxes or sold items on the streets.
- Thousands of children slept rough on the streets – some on the rooftops of London.
- Schooling was not a priority – getting food was!

2 Dr Barnado was so disgusted by the conditions for children that he opened the first home for orphans in 1867. You might have heard of Barnado's!
The Salvation Army also helped poor people by serving food.
Find out more about these two organizations to add to your talk.
Are there places anywhere in the world today where children live like this?

3 Use prompt cards to help you give your talk. Remember you won't be able to read – that would not be a talk!

Connections

Great Expectations has been called a *sensation novel*. This genre was just coming into fashion when Dickens wrote the novel in 1861.

1 What would you guess were the ingredients of a *sensation novel*? Dickens was praised because he had included: suspense, mystery, thrills, cliff-hangers!

2 In order to think about the plot intricacies, fill in the spaces:

_____ is Estella's father, but she's adopted by _____.

Estella's mother is _____ who works for _____.

This man works for _____ and _____. He holds the legal details relating to Pip and _____.

Magwitch was involved with two men: _____ and _____. The former turned out to be Miss Havisham's brother, while the latter was Miss Havisham's _____.

Pip lives most of his childhood with _____ and _____, and thinks he has been given money by _____. However, it is really _____ who has supplied him with money to become a gentleman.

3 Considering all these connections and events, write the blurb for the back of the novel that reflects its position as a *sensation novel*!

Story openings in different styles

1 Discuss the word *genre*. Read the openings below, decide what genre each one could be and highlight the features of text that suggested the genre to you.

> The mist swirled around me. I heard a faint sound of footsteps, dragging through the marshy ground. Metal jangled in the suffocating air. Out of nowhere the figure loomed, arms outstretched, searching for me, reaching for me, overshadowing the ancient gravestones. Nobody to protect me now!

> I have never wanted anyone else. Don't turn away and leave me now that we've found each other again. From the moment I set eyes on you, I knew that I would pursue you.

> Swindling a young lady out of so much cash was an ambitious crime indeed – one that the police would not easily solve. There were too many undercurrents, too many grudges and complications. It wasn't going to be an easy case to crack, but with luck and hard work, they might just do it!

> You may well ask why I sit here, dressed in faded yellow, a grotesque bride, waited on by rodents and decay, waiting for death to take me, whereupon I will settle down to lie on that table – the hard boards will be my bed, no, not my bridal bed. That was long ago. Let me tell you about it . . .

2 In groups of four, choose 4 different genres and write the openings for Dickens's novel. Each one of you will contribute a paragraph, by passing the piece on. Remember to write in the appropriate style. When finished read the pieces aloud to assess your effectiveness.

What's Hulks? Prison-ships

Pip asks what Hulks are and his sister answers prison-ships, but adds, *'People are put in the Hulks because they murder, and because they rob and forge and do all sorts of bad.'*

Hulks were ancient ships that were anchored in the Thames, and at Plymouth and Portsmouth. As prisons became overcrowded, it was decided to use these ships as floating jails.

1 In groups of four, divide into pairs – one will argue for continuing to use Hulks; the other will argue against their use. Each pair will prepare a speech to persuade the class that they are right.

Before writing your speech, think about the rhetorical devices you will use to persuade your audience.

In order to prepare your speech, read the facts on the next sheet, but you will also need to research using your library and the Internet. You might also interview your history teacher who will be able to give you information.

What's Hulks? Prison-ships
continued

Hulks meant that prisons were not too overcrowded.

The conditions for prisoners were tough – the Hulks were filthy and many prisoners died of disease.

Criminals were taken off during the day to, for example, clean sewers. They returned in chains in the evening.

There was very little control and many were killed in violent attacks.

There were about 3,500 prisoners in the ships on the Thames in the early 1840s.

Some prisoners were murderers and some had stolen food, because they were starving.

2 When you have delivered your speech, you might share your views on capital punishment.

Transportation

'You have a returned Transport there, Abel Magwitch.'

With jails becoming more crowded, something had to be done with the criminals. From the early 1700s, they were sent to British colonies. They were taken there and left! This was transportation. Many criminals were violent, but there were men, women and children who had committed petty crimes yet they still received the same sentence.

When it was no longer possible to send prisoners to America (after the War of Independence in the late eighteenth century), the British government looked to Australia.

It was referred to as the New World.

1 Using a map of the world, trace the journey of the first transportation voyage, which went from Britain, to Tenerife, to Brazil, to Cape Town, South Africa and eventually landed in Port Jackson, where a settlement called Sydney was founded.

On a map of Australia, find New South Wales, where Magwitch made a great deal of money working as a sheep-farmer.

2 Using the library and Internet, produce ten facts about Transportation to share with the class. Display your findings so that you have an idea of what it was like for Magwitch and others to be shipped around the world to a strange land.

3 If this happened in the future, perhaps distant planets would be colonized by criminals. With a partner, think about an alien landscape – as fantastical as you want – and describe a 'Transport' stepping out onto the surface for the first time – his feelings and what he sees and hears.

Magwitch's story

1 Magwitch ends up in a prison cell, condemned. Why do you think he risked his life to return to England from New South Wales in Australia? Do you think he was sensible and would you have done that if you had been in his position?

2 From his prison cell, he is going to tell his story. Working in groups of four, the story will unfold – one of you taking the role of Magwitch, talking to an audience, the others miming the key points of his account – getting across the tension and the violence.
Plan the story first, indicating the key points where you will mime the short flashbacks. To plan, you can use a spider diagram, a grid – whatever suits your group best.

- Begin his story with the information on page 43.
- Take the audience back to the first time he met Pip on the marshes – use page 1. You might speculate about how he feels at this point in the telling of it – for example, does he now regret threatening and frightening Pip?
- Move to page 5 and remind the listeners of your surprise when Pip talks of another man.
- Now move forward in your account to the time when you visited Pip in London and surprised him – page 40.
- End your account by explaining how you were captured – page 53.

At this point, develop your use of *physical theatre*. With your bodies form the boat and the river – you will have to consider shape and movement. This type of theatre is effective in producing exciting visual images.

3 Once rehearsed, perform for your class. You might be able to film this, with Magwitch taking centre – talking to camera.

I'm the owner of a London gentleman

1 Who says this and when? What does it suggest to you about money and being able to buy certain things? In groups of four, write down 5 things money can buy, and 5 things money can't possibly buy. Which do you value most? Share ideas with the class.

2 Dickens has a message for his readers. Explain how he encourages us to think about this: **We should not put status and position in society above individual worth.**

In your group, you will create a *sound collage* that emphasises the possibility of it being a *moral fable*. In order to do this, each person will need to have something to say that supports this message. The evidence will be taken from the novel. You will need to choose your words carefully to have maximum impact on your listeners. You might want to use the format of presenting a quotation and commenting on it, for example:

> A: '*This boy! He is a common labouring-boy!*'
>
> B: Pip shouldn't have cared! Estella's opinion was worthless.
>
> A: '*Are you quite sure that you WILL come and see him often?*'
>
> B: He won't. He's ashamed of those who brought him up and cared for him!

If you use this format, deliver the quotations in the appropriate tone to make your point to the listeners. They will make notes on the ideas presented. Once the sound collages are presented, evaluate one (not yours). Use openings like:

> This stressed the idea well, because it . . .
>
> The tone of voice made me . . .

Pip's conscience

1 Work in pairs to decide on adjectives and phrases that describe Pip's character. As you make your decisions, make sure that you have the evidence from the novel to support your choices. Write each one on a card and using a Venn diagram, position the cards in the appropriate places. Share with the class those qualities you think are *positives*, those that are *negatives* and those that are *in between*. Ambition for example could be *in between* – it's good to have ambition like Pip, to want to be a gentleman, but his ambition makes him disloyal to the people who love him and have cared for him over the years.

2 Think about the key changes in Pip. Read pages 24, 25 and 37 and discuss the following quotations:

'The best step I could take towards making myself uncommon was to get out of Biddy everything she knew.' (page 14)

'I had liked it once, but once was not now.' (page 20)

'What I wanted, who can say?' (page 21)

'I would feel more ashamed of home than ever.' (page 21)

'My expectations had done some good to somebody.' (page 38)

'It was for the convict that I had deserted Joe.' (page 41)

'The only good thing I had done.' (page 55)

'I shall never rest until I have worked for the money with which you have kept me out of prison ... Tell me, both, that you can forgive me.' (page 56)

Share your opinions of Pip with the whole class.

Pip's conscience continued

3 Work in pairs. One of you takes the role of Pip; the other of Pip's conscience.
Using the information and opinions gathered, map out important staging points in Pip's story.

Prepare a series of tableaux that depict Pip at these points. As Pip moves from one to the other, the conscience might express his feelings before freezing in position – using your own words or quotations. The conscience then offers advice, at each frozen point, suggesting what Pip should do to be a better person.
Is Pip too passive? Could he have shaped his future?

4 When you have completed the task, perform it for your class. Then evaluate your piece. You might begin:

This worked well, because ...

This part could have been improved by ...

A product of your environment

Many people believe that we are born with personality traits/ characteristics and that no matter where we live, they will remain part of us; whereas some believe that we are shaped by others and our environment, so that our personalities, for example, develop through contact with different surroundings.

Take someone who is evil – perhaps a murderer – is she born evil or is it the way she is brought up and the contacts she has made that have influenced her?

1 In groups, decide what you think of Estella, by jotting down words to describe her appearance and actions. Follow this by describing the surroundings in which she was brought up, then write down who her parents were.

Using this, finish the sentences:

> Pip thought Estella was of a higher status, because....................
>
> She treated Pip ....
>
> He found out that Miss Havisham adopted Estella because she wanted her...........
>
> He also found out that Estella's parents were a .... and a ....

2 Do you feel sorry for Estella? Imagine that you had to defend her against accusations of being: unfeeling, hard-hearted, mean and deceptive.

Write the speech you will give to your class who will act as 'the jury' deciding whether she can be excused because of her upbringing or whether she should be blamed totally for her behaviour. Remember what Pip said on page 19: 'What could I become with these surroundings? How could my character fail to be influenced by them?'

A touch of realism

1 What word can you see inside the word *realism*? How does that help you work out the definition?

2 In many stories, authors use real places in order to make the story appear more realistic. Dickens uses this technique. He sets scenes in places in Britain that his readers would have recognized. They are also familiar to us.

On a map of Britain, locate the following: the county of Kent, London and in London – Smithfield, Hammersmith, Soho, Essex Street.

In what countries are: New South Wales, the cities of Hamburg and Rotterdam?

Can you remember who lived in Kent? Who lived in London? Who went to New South Wales and why? Why are the European cities important?

What do we learn of London from the text? Read pages 28, 32, 46, 47, 48 to help you gain some detail.

A touch of realism continued

3 Read the extract below from the original text.

> I came to Smithfield – the shameful place, all asmear with filth and fat and blood and foam. I saw the great black dome of Saint Paul's bulging at me from behind a grim stone building which a bystander said was Newgate Prison. I found the roadway covered with straw to deaden the noise of the passing vehicles, and from this and from the quantity of people standing about, smelling strongly of spirits and beer, I inferred that the trials were on. A partially drunk minister of justice was so good as to take me into a yard and show me where the gallows was kept and also where people were publicly whipped and then he showed me the Debtors' Door, out of which culprits came to be hanged.

Now answer the following:

- What does the list: '*filth and fat and blood and foam*' suggest to you?
- Think about our five senses: touch, sight, smell, taste, and hearing – find examples in the text that make us use these senses, for example, '*I saw the great black dome*'.
- What colours are suggested to you and what effect do these colours have on the reader?
- What do you think Dickens meant by: '*the minister of justice was so good as to take me into a yard*'. Do you think he meant *good* or was he implying the opposite? If so, what techniques is he using?
- What impression do you get of London?

4 Describe a part of your town or city so that it appeals to strangers. Use positive adjectives and phrases that make your reader want to visit this area.

Let your partner read it so that you can compare your work and check the effectiveness of your word choices and style.

Autobiography

1 What does the prefix *auto* signify? Can you think of other words that begin with it?

2 In this case, Pip is writing his life story up to a certain point and he writes it in *the first person singular – 'I'*.

His story begins: 'My father's family name being Pirrip . . .'

His is not the only story told. In the original text, Magwitch says:

> 'I am not going to tell you my life, like a song or story-book. But to give it to you short and handy, I'll put it at once into a mouthful of English. In jail and out of jail, in jail and out of jail. There, you've got it. Tramping, begging, thieving, working sometimes, a bit of a poacher, labourer, waggoner, haymaker . . .'

Herbert tells part of Miss Havisham's story; Jaggers tells Pip something of Estella's mother's story.

And all of these are reported by Pip.

3 In groups of four, choose one character from the novel. Write a paragraph relating to an important event in the life of that person. Pass the paragraph to another group, who must then improvise the event.

4 The whole class, directed by your teacher, might try to improvise the search for the convicts at the beginning – using no words, but using actions to illustrate: the two convicts running, the soldiers tracking them, the crowd following with Joe and Pip, the capture and the crowd watching as they are chained and taken away.

Pip's scrapbook

Great Expectations is a story about Pip growing up. Pip tells it in the first person singular.

1 Many children and adults keep a scrapbook of things that remind them of growing up, moving on from one place to another. If you have kept a scrapbook, discuss with a partner what types of things you have stuck in it! If not, what types of things might others preserve in them?

Did you come up with tickets, feathers, postcards, photographs? What else?

2 Read the list below and explain why Pip might want to keep some of these things. What might they remind him of?
What might they tell us about his character?

- a ticket for a pantomime
- a pressed bridal flower
- a playing card
- two one-pound notes
- an invitation to dinner
- a letter from Biddy

Think of other items that Pip might stick in his scrapbook and explain your choices.

Names and identities

1 Why is your name important to you? Do you have a nickname? If so, who do you 'allow' to use it? Do your parents call you something other than your full name?

2 Names are an important part of our identity and they play a significant role in this novel.
To help you consider this, answer the following questions:

- Why does Pip call himself this (page 1)?
- What is the difference between being called *boy* by Estella and Miss Havisham (page 11) and being called *boy* by the convict (page 43)?
- Why does Pip call Herbert the 'pale young gentleman' and Herbert call Pip 'the prowling boy?'
- Why has the convict assumed a different name from his own (page 42)?
- What does Pip tell Herbert is the relationship between the convict and himself and why does Pip go shopping (page 42)?
- Why does Wemmick call the convict: Tom, Jack or Richard (page 46)?

3 Names might deceive, but Estella also says: 'Do you want me to deceive and entrap you?'
Why does Estella deceive men?
Who do you think Pip deceives the most, that is, until he matures and realizes who is really important?

Names and identities continued

4 Can you think of other times in the story when deceit, lies, or a covering up of the whole truth has taken place? What is the writer trying to tell us about the way in which we deceive ourselves and others?

In order to write a response, you might use the following paragraph openings:

Names are very important to us, because they are part of our identity. On the first page of the novel, . . .

The way in which characters talk to each other shows their attitudes and their sense of their own status, for example, the word 'boy' is used . . .

To avoid recapture, the convict has to change his name and appearance, but although he is a criminal, underneath he . . .

Unlike Magwitch, Estella is a woman of high class, but she has been conditioned by Miss Havisham to . . .

Joe and Biddy never try to hide their identities. They are . . .

Appearances can be deceiving. Pip deceives himself and it is only at the end . . .

To sum up, Dickens might have wanted his readers to think about names, identities and how they can deceive. The lesson I think he wanted us to learn is . . .

Joe Gargery

Joe is a sympathetic character who brings a lot of humour to the story.

1 In deciding why readers like Joe, collect key words that describe his qualities. Share your ideas with the class.

2 Working in pairs, prepare to mime the action in the following scenes, using your facial expressions, gestures and body language to illustrate how much Joe cares for Pip and others. At the end of each mime, freeze before moving on. This will allow your class to suggest what emotions Joe is experiencing at this time.

- protecting Pip from Tickler and Mrs Joe (page 3)
- watching Pip as he thinks he's bolting his food (page 3)
- accepting the convict's apology for stealing food (page 8)
- feeling embarrassed in London with Pip (pages 33, 34)
- caring for Pip (page 55)
- forgiving Pip – if he has anything to forgive (page 56)

3 Some things he says make us smile. Try to explain why:
'Joe mustered courage to propose that some if us should go with the soldiers' (page 7); *'he took us home and hammered us. Which were a drawback on my learning'* (page 9); *'Mrs Joe musn't see what we're up to'* (page 9); *'That ain't the way to get out of being common'* (page 13)
Find other examples where we smile at his words and actions.

4 Collect the words and phrases you have used to describe Joe. In the role of Biddy, explain what it was about this man that made you want to marry him.

Biddy

1 Look at the snippets of diary entries below. These are all taken from Biddy's diary.
Find the event each one of them refers to. Decide what the event / conversation tells you about Biddy's character.

> Pip's been to Miss H. It seems he wants to make himself uncommon. He's asked me to teach him.

> Poor old Joe and Pip. The least I can do is offer to care for Mrs Joe until we can sort things out.

> I'm worried what with Pip and his ambitions. I think he wants to be a gentleman for all the wrong reasons. I've offered my advice, but I'm not sure he'll take it. He's not sensible – I know he'll never be able to love me, no matter what he thinks he wants.

> He says he'll visit Joe often. I can see in his eyes that he won't. I know him better than he knows himself. I asked him if he really would come, but he didn't realize what I was suggesting.

> Joe is caring for Pip in London. I am so pleased that we can help him through this hard time – with money and kindness.

> He asked for forgiveness! What's to forgive? He'll always be in our hearts.

2 In the role of Biddy's friend – one whom she confides in – write the script in which you talk about Pip and all that has happened.

Hot-seating Pip

1 *Hot-seat* is a term used in Drama. What does the word mean?

2 If you had the chance to meet Pip, there would be a number of things you might like to say to him and a number of questions you might like to ask.

In pairs, you are going to decide what questions you would like to put to Pip.

One member of your class will take on the role of Pip. That pupil must remind himself of events from the story, the emotions Pip went through and the regrets he might have.

You are not out to trick the person who is in the role of Pip. You are giving that pupil an opportunity to explore Pip's character with you. Once you have completed your questions, be prepared to ask them. The pupil in the role of Pip will answer.

3 In groups, using the information found during the hot-seating and using your own opinions, list a time: when you think Pip acted foolishly, when he was mean, when he was brave, when he realized how badly he had behaved.

4 Prepare a short piece in which you tell him exactly what you think of him and his past behaviour! You might perform this for the class. Is Pip a sympathetic character?

A sad reflection on humanity

1 Read the following sentences and, in pairs, decide whom they are describing:

- A criminal who wants to own a gentleman.
- A young man who rejects his loving family because he is ashamed of them.
- A bitter old woman who adopts a baby to raise her to wreak revenge on men.
- A deceiving young lady who has a heart of ice.
- A swindler who cheats on a woman, jilting her on her wedding day.
- A workman who batters a woman, thus causing her death.
- A brother who takes part in a plan to cheat his sister and ruin her life.

All of these characters play a major role in the novel's plot.

2 Would you say, on reading *only* this information, that the novel is a pessimistic or optimistic one? Does this information truthfully reflect the people who exist in the novel? In pairs, argue the case that this novel is an optimistic one.
You will need to examine the way in which some of these characters change.

3 When you have your reasons prepared, rehearse your piece, before presenting it to the class.

Different text types

1 Read the different text types below. Decide what they are and highlight those features that helped you to decide. Each piece might have been spoken/written by a character or might represent their thoughts. Explain how you worked things out.

> I can't let 'im take the blame. He brought me wittles and a file. I'll say I stole. Won't harm me to do that now.

> What fun to be able to tease and torment these foolish men! Pip's face when he spoke to me of Drummle! But there is something about Pip – I could not deceive or entrap him, though this is for these pages alone. I would not share that with Miss Havisham.

> Joe, I think he will be glad to see you. I'll write that in here shall I? I'll tell him we talk of him every night. But he might be changed now that he is becoming a gentleman.

> I bear witness to the fact that Mr Jaggers has duly informed Mr Philip Pirrip of the financial arrangements. The client is aware of the allowance and has been informed of the fact that he will have dealings with myself – Mr . . .

2 Choose two different text types. Write extracts from them as if you are characters in the novel. Swap with your partner. How easy is it to guess correctly?

I never saw my father and mother

Pip says this on the opening page of the novel. Immediately we feel sympathy for him.

1 But he isn't the only one who has never seen his parents or who has uncaring parents.
What about Pip's sister? And Estella? Joe also talks about his parents on page 9 – what kind of father did he have?

2 Dickens often wrote about the situations children lived in. Which other of his novels do you know in which he writes about children? Research in your library to find out what happened to the following: Oliver Twist, Tiny Tim, David Copperfield.
Try an experiment – ask a number of older people to name one of Dickens's fictional children – probably all of them will be able to name one!

3 Even in today's world we see children living in appalling conditions. Many charities raise funds to help them. Can you name any?

4 Again, research into Children's Charities – Dr Barnado, for example, set up the first homes for orphans in 1867. Examine the publicity material that these charities use – looking specifically at the language of persuasion and the use of visual images.
Using your findings, design a poster or write a leaflet that asks the reader to donate money to the chosen charity.

5 Compare your techniques by swapping work in a group of four. Evaluate your pieces using sentence openings, such as:

This made me feel guilty, because …

This was eye-catching, because s/he used …

To improve s/he could have …

Expectations!

1 Jaggers, the lawyer, tells Pip on page 26 that he is to be brought up as 'a gentleman of great expectations'.
What do you understand by this phrase? In pairs, discuss what expectations you have in life.

2 The characters in the novel all have different expectations. Some are prepared to work hard for their future, whereas some would prefer to use others; some are content to live a simple life, while others have ambitions, not always good ones!
Answer the following:

- Which three men hoped to gain money through a scam/swindle?
- Who was content to live life simply, in a small house in the Kent marshland?
- Who wasn't happy with his situation and constantly wanted to be what he considered 'better'?
- Who expected to use another to gain revenge on men?

3 Many characters are preoccupied with money – what message do you think Dickens is putting across when he explores the different lives and ambitions in this novel?

4 Who would you say were the happiest characters in the story? Whose life would you find the most acceptable if you had to choose. Give clear reasons for your choice.

The pale young gentleman

1 In order to write about Herbert Pocket's character, you will need to read the relevant pages in the book. Work in pairs. Take notes showing what kind of a person Herbert is.

You must find evidence from the story to support your points. You must draw out the qualities Herbert shows during the story, for example:

Story/evidence	Qualities
He tries to help Magwitch escape	loyalty to Pip, true friendship and bravery.

Read pages 18, 29, 30, 31, 43, 46, 47, 53, 56 – making your notes.

2 On cards, write down the qualities you have decided Herbert has – these can be expressed in phrases or you might write just one word, for example, he shows loyalty or Loyalty. On another set of cards, write down the evidence from the novel.

3 Pass your cards to another pair. They must match up the 'quality cards' with the appropriate 'evidence cards'.

And they both lived happily ever after

1 This is a formulaic line that you must have read so many times. In what genre would you find it? Read the ending of *Great Expectations* again. Does it suggest happiness?

2 This was not the original ending. The first draft saw Pip walking along a street in London with little Pip (Biddy and Joe's son); Estella was to have been married a second time to a doctor and it read like this:

> I was walking along Piccadilly with little Pip when a servant came running after me to ask would I step back to a lady in a carriage who wished to speak to me … the lady and I looked sadly enough on one another. 'I am greatly changed, I know; but I thought you would like to shake hands with Estella too, Pip. Lift up that pretty child and let me kiss it!' (She supposed the child, I think, to be my child.) I was very glad afterwards to have had the interview; for, in her face and in her voice, and in her touch, she gave me the assurance, that suffering had been stronger than Miss Havisham's teaching and had given her a heart to understand what my heart used to be.

Which ending do you prefer, if any? Dickens thought the ending we have now was 'more acceptable' – why might he have felt that?

3 Read page 58 again. What does the word *'solitary'* suggest together with there being no Satis House, only the garden wall? Why are the mists rising at the end and what does the *'shadow'* represent?

4 Do Pip and Estella end up together or is this ambiguous? If you have a more acceptable idea, write your own ending, sharing it with a partner.